AuthorHouse™
1663 Liberty Drive
Bloomington, IN 47403
www.authorhouse.com
Phone: 833-262-8899

This book is printed on acid-free paper.

ISBN: 978-1-4208-9412-7 (sc)

Library of Congress Control Number: 2005909365

Print information available on the last page.

Published by AuthorHouse 04/05/2023

authorHOUSE°

Thanks to my family.

I see the moon from afar.
It's Eid.

First our family will go to the mosque to pray.

We will hear that Eid-ul-Fitr marks the end of Ramadan. It celebrates the month when Muslims fast. They give thanks for the holy book, the Quran.

My father gives money to the mosque.

Then we hug family and friends.

They come to my house for Eid breakfast.

My mother sets the table.

My sisters come downstairs in their new clothes.

We all eat parathas and chicken.
I pass out the kebab.

My aunt fries more parathas
and serves firni.

After breakfast the children play games. Pictionary is my favorite.

My sister's team wins the game.

It's time to exchange presents.

My uncles and aunts give the children money.

My little cousins sing and dance.

We take a family picture.
Everyone smiles with joy.

Author's Note

Eid-ul-Fitr marks the completion of fasting during Ramadan. It celebrates the month in which the holy Quran was first revealed to Prophet Mohammad (PBUH). The holiday takes place in the tenth month of the Islamic calendar. The sighting of the moon confirms the celebration of Eid-ul-Fitr. It is a time of gratitude and helping others. Initially, over a billion Muslims perform a special prayer. They give a donation called zakat-ul-fitr. This amount is paid according to one's wealth. It is used to help individuals in need. Further, Muslims hug and greet each other with the phrase "Eid Mubarak," which means Happy Eid. Family and friends continue the day with social visits. They exchange gifts and share traditional foods. Some countries eat parathas—flat bread—and firni—rice pudding.

Printed in the United States
by Baker & Taylor Publisher Services